YOUR KNOWLEDGE HAS VALUE

- We will publish your bachelor's and
  master's thesis, essays and papers

- Your own eBook and book -
  sold worldwide in all relevant shops

- Earn money with each sale

Upload your text at www.GRIN.com
and publish for free

Ben Wagner

Mitt Romney - Using Technology To Spread His Vision

GRIN Verlag

Bibliografische Information der Deutschen Nationalbibliothek:

Die Deutsche Bibliothek verzeichnet diese Publikation in der Deutschen National-
bibliografie; detaillierte bibliografische Daten sind im Internet über http://dnb.d-
nb.de/ abrufbar.

Imprint:

Copyright © 2012 GRIN Verlag GmbH
Druck und Bindung: Books on Demand GmbH, Norderstedt Germany
ISBN: 978-3-656-14789-3

This book at GRIN:

http://www.grin.com/en/e-book/190264/mitt-romney-using-technology-to-spread-
his-vision

Mitt Romney

Using Technology To Spread His Vision

Mid Term Paper

Comm 466

Written By: Ben Wagner

March 6, 2012

Table Of Contents

Abstract

The forces of technology are ever changing. In each of our own lives, we have seen the transition from using the fax machine, to e-mail, to texting, and now using Twitter and a variety of other social media outlets to give us voice and make our messages known. We may have let many of these transitions go unnoticed over the years, but as we stop and think about how they have affected us, or someone else, it is remarkable to see the stark contrasts that do exist. This paper will examine the lie and changing times of Mitt Romney, the current Front Runner in the Republican Party Presidential Nomination process.

This paper will examine the days of Mitt's youth though adulthood and focus on not only how his environment influenced his rearing, but also how the use of technology changed the path of his life in Business as well as Politics. Many of the principals examined in this document will be easy to relate to, as many of us have experienced personally the technological changes that will be discussed. The fast pace of technological change has different impacts on each of us, but all of us will be able to take some kind of appreciation from this reading and have a better understanding of the role technology plays in our live. Both seen, as well as unseen.

Romney Family History

Willard Mitt Romney was born into this world on March 12, 1947 to a well established and successful home in the state of Michigan. His parents, George W. Romney, and Lenore Romney, had not always enjoyed the life of wealth that they had established by the time Mitt came into their home. George was born in Mexico and had dual citizenship within the United States as well. At a young age, his parents moved to the United States to seek better living conditions for their family. For much of George's life, even well into adulthood, he struggled financially and was forced to move several times to seek employment that would be suitable for his family's needs.

Lenore was born in Logan, Utah, to a family that did not struggle in terms of wealth (Boston). She and George met in high school and after a lengthy courtship that included George traveling coast to coast to stay near Lenore, they were married in 1931. Mitt was born at a time when his father had made himself a success by working in the automobile marketplace. Mitt was placed in normal conditions for the first several years of his education, attending public school through his Junior high years, at which point his parents placed him in a private school (Crimson). This decision was made in part to his father's move into the political arena, which happened Mitt's sophomore year of High School.

Being Raised In Politics

In 1962, George Romney left his position at American Motor Cars, where he was a chief executive, and formed a campaign for the Gubernatorial race in the state of Michigan (NY Times). During this time in Mitt's life, he experienced his first taste of what running a political campaign was all about. Due to the limited technology of the time, that campaign was ran in such a way that done alone, would not produce great results in our current time. George spent much time traveling across Michigan, meeting voters and shaking hands while giving speeches to small groups throughout the state.

Mitt was not used as a main cog in the political machine of that political contest. He was very willing and eager to assist in whatever way he could. It is noted that at a State Fair in Michigan, he took the podium and shared a message of trust he had in his father, stating "he will make things better!" (Time). To make a small note, Mitt Romney is utilizing his son's in a much more active way than his father did, namely because his children are much older than Mitt was at the time of his father's election. As Mitt did mature and get older, his father appointed him to positions of higher prestige within his campaign and framework. Mitt served as an intern for the Governor's office and was present at key political moments in the history of our Nation, such as the 1964 Republican National Convention (Deseret).

Mitt gained invaluable memories from these early times in his life. He watched his father and took note of the confidence he always held, at the power behind the speeches he gave, and at the admiration others had towards his father. He knew from a young age that he wanted to take those traits that would help him through life by being able to work well with others. In contrast to the young life of Mitt Romney, too few young people today have the opportunity to learn these key social skills, due in part to the advent of social media. So much of our communication, especially of those of the younger generation, is done informally though the means of electronic communication. Several studies have shown that the young people of today are lacking in strong social skills, with the root cause being blamed on social media (APA). Mitt was able to further enhance his people skills as he served a 30 month religious mission for the LDS church, meeting people everyday and speaking to them in a language that was not his native tongue. He also dealt with the challenge of only being able to communicate with his family and friends through the medium of writing letters, with the exception of 2 phone calls home a year, on Christmas and Mother's Day. All of these situations further enhanced his understanding of the importance of communication as well as his skills gaining trust of others.

Incorporating Available Technologies

After gaining valuable skills in the realm of leadership from his College years as well as entering into marriage with his High School sweetheart Ann and having his first two children, Mitt stepped into the corporate world to make his mark in business. After spending some time working with Boston Consulting Group, Romney was recruited to join a new firm called Bain Capital. One of the major reasons he was sought after by the firm's founder was due to the fact that "He had the appearance of confidence of a guy who was maybe ten years older." (NY Times 2). The maturity and knowledge that Romney possessed was in part thanks to his early experiences spending time around people of influence while his father was Governor as well as the maturity he gained during his time out of the country spreading Christianity.

Romney and his business associates kept current on the available technologies, just as most business leaders do. He wanted to do all he could to use these technologies to their advantage to bring more money to the bottom line and make their venture more profitable. Mitt has been known for his position on what good technological advancement provides in the world of business, and he has done all in his power to always ride "the curve" of technology throughout his business life (Issues).

Salt Lake City Winter Olympics

In February of 1999, Mitt received an offer to become the President of the Salt Lake Organizing Committee for the Olympic and Paralympic Winter Games of 2002. This was a fortunate situation for him, because his wife had been diagnosed with Multiple Sclerosis one year earlier, and had found an effective treatment regimen that she was able to achieve at their home in Park City, Utah, which is within an hour of downtown Salt Lake City (NY Times 3). Romney used his newly found position of prominence to not only make the winter games a success, but also to shine up his own image, further preparing him for a life in the public eye that he had sought in the past unsuccessfully. Mitt was intentional about making and appearance for countless photo opprotunities as well as several television and radio ads promoting the games and urging citizens around the world to come to Utah and enjoy the Winter Games in the "Heart of the Rocky Mountains" (NY Times 3).

Another avenue of communication that Mitt successfully incorporated into the games was in the world of advertising. Mitt, knowing the far reaching consequences of effective communication in all its forms, aggressively sought corporate sponsors to help fund the games that year, which had been in dire economic straights until Romney was brought on board. The chairmen of the Salt Lake Winter Games was Robert H. Garff, who once stated about Mitt "It was obvious that he had an agenda larger than just the Olympics" (NY Times 3). Mitt took advantage of his time in this role to prove to himself and anyone who wanted to see, that he was a proven leader, an effective communicator, a "shameless" promoter, and a visionary. All of these attributes served him well as he dusted off the embarrassment from his one time United States Senate Campaign trying to take the seat of longtime Senator Ted Kennedy and went home to Massachusetts to take a stab at gaining the states highest office.

Massachusetts Gubernatorial Campaign

Upon successful completion of the Winter Olympic Games in early 2002, Romney found his next avenue of power, the Governorship of the state of Massachusetts, where he had lived and operated his business for some 20 years. He ran as a Republican, facing two female opponents who represented the Democratic and Green Parties respectively. He faced opposition almost immediately after his announcement to make a run of office, with the states' Democratic Party objecting to his citizenship in that state, citing that he had claimed full time residency in the state of Utah for the past 3 years. However, that opposition was never sustained due to the fact that he had maintained property in Massachusetts and had paid taxes to the state even while living in Utah (NY Times 4).

Due to Mitt's wealth and experience, which he tried to use as an advantage over his competitors, he was attacked by the other parties for being "out of touch with the people of Massachusetts". He quickly turned that argument into one of his greatest strengths in his campaign, focusing on his success in business and his ability to cut waste and maximize efficiency of processes, which in his opinion would be easily transferable to the public sector. His campaign was the first in this race to focus on what turned out to be an effective mode of communication with the voters, his campaign began employing micro targeting. Micro targeting is going after a very specific demographic of voter, and presenting a message tailored directly at them (Usgovt). In an effort led by Carl Gage, the founder of a national polling service, Mitt was intentional and deliberate with the use of his message to each group he targeted (Washington).

The main objective of this was to target independent voters, determine what issues were important to them, and campaign to those wants and desires through an effective media campaign as well as personal speeches delivered to groups where it was well known there were independent voters (Washington). Through their efforts, they were able to collect data that showed that not all independent voters were focused on the same issues. According to Michael Murphy, who was serving as a key strategist for the Romney campaign, they found " That a 32-year-old white Protestant woman with two children and a retired Roman Catholic male engineer -- while both independents -- were driven by often contradictory issues. Some independents are more base Republican -- like, some are pure fiscal [voters], some are focused on education" (Washington).

Having this specific data proved to be invaluable to the longevity of the campaign. Romney won the race capturing 49.77% of the popular vote. Among independent voters, he was able to gain the support of a majority of them in the mainstream areas of the state, while holding even with independents in smaller, more rural areas of the state where his campaign was less focused (Washington). Once in office, Mitt continued to use advocate the advancement in technology and education, and utilized minimally the Internet to reach out to the citizens of his state. Towards the end of a successful one term, he announced that he had no intent on running for re-election, a move that caused his popularity ratings to take a hard hit in the state. He did, however, on his last day in office announce his intentions to form an Exploratory Committee to make a run for President of The United States.

Lessons From 2008 Presidential Campaign

On January 5th, 2007, Governor Mitt Romney stepped out of office in Massachusetts and entered right into the new venture that a day prior he had announced, that of forming an exploratory committee flirting with running for the highest office in the land. After making several stops throughout the country giving speeches touting his conservative values and track records, he formally announced his candidacy in February 2007. In that same month, Mitt entered the arena of promoting his message through the medium of technological communication.

Advertisements hit the airwaves of television and radio in several media markets throughout the country, with an emphasis on some of the early primary and caucus states such as New Hampshire and Iowa (NY Times 5). Mitt also did something that is still considered very untraditional in a national election, he took his message to the Cable Television airwaves, to get the message out of who he was and what he stood for. Many of the other candidates running that year were better known on a national basis such as John McCain and Rudy Giuliani, so his campaign felt it was wise to spend a substantial amount of campaign cash to air ads in states that wouldn't be holding Primary or Caucuses for up to 15months later (NY Times 5). As Alex Castellanos, a strategist for the Romney 2008 campaign, said "Every campaign has different needs and different jobs, someone who's unknown has an opportunity to be introduced" (NY Times 5).

This advertising did pay off. Mitt held a substantial lead in many of the early polls and gained momentum from picking up key endorsements from big time political figures within the GOP. Not only did he focus on hitting a national audience through the use of technology, but he also hadn't forgotten the value that a handshake and greeting will hold with a potential voter, lessons that he learned at a young age watching his father campaign for office during a more "simple" time in America. Mitt held rallies titled "Ask Mitt Anything", an opportunity for people all over America to get their personal question answered, whether it was concerning his religion or his views on subsidies given to farmers in this country (NY Times 5).

Like Mitt had done for his father George, he employed the help of his 5 sons, Tagg, Matt, Josh, Ben, and Craig to venture out together and tell the people of this country a little about their family and to express their views and experiences with their father. The Romney campaign even went as far as to charter a tour bus and titled it "The Five Brothers Bus" and sent the brothers throughout the 99 counties of Iowa, meeting the voters and warming them up to the idea of giving their father a shot to be the next President of The United States (CBS).

Just as Mitt understood the power of communication by means of Television broadcast, so too did all of his competitors, who ran hefty attack ads on Mitt covering subjects as varied as His tenure as Governor, to his time as Olympic President. The televised debates, which are another tool Romney tried to utilize to maintain his public image, became more of a boxing match among him and his 2 chief rivals Senator John McCain and Former Arkansas Governor Mike Huckabee. Ultimately, Mitt conceded in February of 2008, endorsing Senator John McCain that same month. Although defeated in that particular battle, Romney learned valuable information about himself and how campaigns run on a National level. Mitt was proud of the campaign he had ran and the fact that his campaign brought in the most fund-raising money of any of the Republican candidates, and he quietly slipped aside for a time to plan his next move.

Romney 2.0 - The 2012 Presidential Campaign

Dusting himself off and reviewing the lessons learned from the last round of campaigning, Mitt approached his wife and sought her approval to make another Presidential run. Ann Romney had mixed feelings on the subject, as I am sure any wife would, especially one who still suffered from a battle with multiple sclerosis. She posed one question to him, "I asked Mitt if you are able to be the nominee of the party and if you are able to beat Barack Obama, I don't want to go through all this and when you get there not be able to fix it. I need you to answer me this, can you fix it; and he said he could" (Northwest). On June 2, 2011, Mitt formally announced the start of his campaign.

There were several differences this time around. Having the advantage of name recognition this time around, he didn't spend so many resources spreading his image across the cable airwaves coast to coast. Instead, he went with a much cheaper approach, that was far more reaching, Facebook and Twitter. Utilizing the power of social media has been a game changer for Mitt this time around. As Heather Dougherty of Experian Hitwise stated recently, "While these measures alone are not enough to secure the nomination, this is a positive sign for the Romney campaign that social efforts are gaining attention and building an audience on Facebook" (PC). As recently as last month, Mitt's Facebook page had seen a 248% increase in visitors and his site was being visited 1.7 times more than Ron Paul'ss' (who has been maintaining anon-linene presence longer) and 2.5 times more than President Obama's page, which as of March 5 2012 has 25,450,903 "Likes" compared to Romney's 1,510,595 "Likes" (Facebook).

Mitt's campaign has also maintained an active Twitter account, averaging 6-9 "Tweets" Daily. Twitter has proved to also be a stumbling block in the Romney campaign. After a gaffe made in December in which Romney bet Texas Governor Rick Perry $10,000 over a point in one of Romney's books, the "Twitterverse" went wild with mentions of Romney and how he is out of touch with the common man making such a large bet (Talking). There is still plenty of old fashion travel and meet and greets included in addition to a strong on-line presence from Mitt, but its safe to say that his success thus far has come in part due to his newly found on-line voice.

Conclusion

From our examination of the life and times of Mitt Romney, it is safe to say that technology in a short 65 years has exploded into a mad rush to stay current with all the latest trends and topics. While radio communication was a large part of George Romney's campaign days, we now see that Mitt is having to keep up with social communication via technological advances to stay relevant and current. If the past trends are any indicator of the future role that technology plays in communication in political contests, then it is safe to say that those who will one day run for office in the future had better be prepared to make full use of every available communication resource at their disposal or risk becoming lost in a world of ever changing communication technologies.

Works Cited

Belluck, Pam. "Massachusetts Ballot Panel Allows Race By Republican." *The New York Times*. The New York Times, 26 June 2002. Web. 05 Mar. 2012. <http://www.nytimes.com/2002/06/26/us/massachusetts-ballot-panel-allows-race-by-republican.html>.

Chessum, Jake. 10 May 2007. Web. 5 Mar. 2012. <http://www.time.com/time/magazine/article/0,9171,1619536,00.html>.

Facebook. 05 Mar. 2012. Web. 05 Mar. 2012. <https://www.facebook.com/index.php?lh=5c599d2970d275a65fd9dd23e7c2577a&#;!/mittromney>.

Hazelwood, Blaise. "Romney's Data Cruncher." *Washington Post*. The Washington Post, 05 July 2007. Web. 05 Mar. 2012. <http://www.washingtonpost.com/wp-dyn/content/article/2007/07/04/AR2007070401423_2.html>.

Horn, Leslie. "Mitt Romney Leads GOP Presidential Race (on Facebook)." *PCMAG*. 24 Jan. 2012. Web. 05 Mar. 2012. <http://www.pcmag.com/article2/0,2817,2399296,00.asp>.

Johnson, Kirk. "In Olympics Success, Romney Found New Edge." 19 Sept. 2007. Web. 3 Mar. 2012. <http://www.nytimes.com/2007/09/19/us/politics/19romney.html?_r=2&pagewanted=all>.

Kirkpatrick, David A. "Romney's Fortunes Tied to Business Riches." 4 June 2007. Web. 5 Mar. 2012. <http://www.nytimes.com/2007/06/04/us/politics/04bain.html?_r=1>.

Luo, Michael. "Romney Steps Up Advertising Push." 13 June 2007. Web. 5 Mar. 2012. <http://www.nytimes.com/2007/06/13/us/politics/13ads.html>.

"Mitt Romney's $10,000 Bet Blows Up Twitter." *Mitt Romney $10,000 Bet Blows Up Twitter*. Web. 05 Mar. 2012. <http://2012.talkingpointsmemo.com/2011/12/mitt-romneys-10000-bet-blows-up-twitter.php>.

"Mitt Romney on the Issues." *Object Moved*. Web. 05 Mar. 2012. <http://www.issues2000.org/Mitt_Romney.htm>.

"NEWS." *The Harvard Crimson*. Web. 05 Mar. 2012. <http://www.thecrimson.com/article/1994/10/21/romney-gains-momentum-as-he-keeps/>.

"Privilege, Tragedy, and a Young Leader." Web. 5 Mar. 2012.

    <http://www.boston.com/news/politics/2008/specials/romney/articles/part1_mai n/>.

"Romney: Sons Serve Country By Campaigning." *CBSNews*. CBS Interactive, 11 Feb. 2009. Web. 05 Mar. 2012.

    <http://www.cbsnews.com/stories/2007/08/08/politics/main3147321.shtml>.

Rosen, Larry. "Social Networking's Good and Bad Impacts on Kids." *American Psychological Association (APA)*. 6 Aug. 2011. Web. 05 Mar. 2012.

    <http://www.apa.org/news/press/releases/2011/08/social-kids.aspx>.

Rosenbaum, David E. "George Romney Dies at 88; A Leading G.O.P. Figure." *The New York Times*. The New York Times, 27 July 1995. Web. 05 Mar. 2012.

    <http://www.nytimes.com/1995/07/27/obituaries/george-romney-dies-at-88-a-leading-gop-figure.html>.

Swidey, Neil. "Mitt Romney: The Begining." 1 July 2007. Web. 5 Mar. 2012.

    http://web.archive.org/web/20070918090328/http://deseretnews.com/dn/view/0, 1249,6 80195540,00.html>.

"US Government Teachers Blog." *: Microtargeting*. 29 Jan. 2012. Web. 05 Mar. 2012.

    <http://usgovteducatorsblog.blogspot.com/2012/01/microtargeting.html>.

Wiggens, Hubert. "Mitt Romney Makes His First Campaign Stop in Toledo." 29 Feb. 2012. Web. 5 Mar. 2012.

    <http://www.northwestohio.com/news/story.aspx?id=725164>.